James Porter

Clergyman's Pocket Diary and Visiting Book

Volume 1

James Porter

Clergyman's Pocket Diary and Visiting Book
Volume 1

ISBN/EAN: 9783337126094

Printed in Europe, USA, Canada, Australia, Japan

Cover: Foto ©Lupo / pixelio.de

More available books at **www.hansebooks.com**

CLERGYMAN'S

POCKET DIARY

AND

VISITING BOOK

18

ARRANGED BY

JAMES PORTER, D.D.

REVISED EDITION

NEW YORK: EATON & MAINS
CINCINNATI: CURTS & JENNINGS

EATON & MAINS PRESS,
150 Fifth Avenue, New York.

PREFACE.

THE object of this manual is to furnish our Pastors with a Pocket Diary, Visiting Book, and Church Directory in one volume. It is so arranged that it may answer their purpose two years if necessary. Hence we have omitted the unit in the figures representing the year except in the Calendar. Those who wish to use the book more than two years can do so by pasting in a new Calendar. We have also omitted the letters from the Diary indicating the day of the week, for the same reason. Thus the preachers have, in small compass, the information which they need in acting as agents for books and periodicals and the benevolent societies of the Church.

It is not presumed that the book will please everyone. Some will regret that we did not insert *this*, and others that we omitted *that*. But it must be remembered that the work is designed to be carried in the pocket always and everywhere, and if made to embrace too much it would be too large, and so complex as not fully to answer the purpose contemplated.

The blanks left for an index can be filled so as readily to find any memorandum that may be made.

PUBLISHERS.

CALENDAR.

1897

	Sunday.	Monday.	Tuesday.	Wednesday.	Thursday.	Friday.	Saturday.
JAN.						1	2
	3	4	5	6	7	8	9
	10	11	12	13	14	15	16
	17	18	19	20	21	22	23
	24	25	26	27	28	29	30
	31						
FEB.		1	2	3	4	5	6
	7	8	9	10	11	12	13
	14	15	16	17	18	19	20
	21	22	23	24	25	26	27
	28						
MAR.		1	2	3	4	5	6
	7	8	9	10	11	12	13
	14	15	16	17	18	19	20
	21	22	23	24	25	26	27
	28	29	30	31			
APRIL					1	2	3
	4	5	6	7	8	9	10
	11	12	13	14	15	16	17
	18	19	20	21	22	23	24
	25	26	27	28	29	30	
MAY							1
	2	3	4	5	6	7	8
	9	10	11	12	13	14	15
	16	17	18	19	20	21	22
	23	24	25	26	27	28	29
	30	31					
JUNE			1	2	3	4	5
	6	7	8	9	10	11	12
	13	14	15	16	17	18	19
	20	21	22	23	24	25	26
	27	28	29	30			
JULY					1	2	3
	4	5	6	7	8	9	10
	11	12	13	14	15	16	17
	18	19	20	21	22	23	24
	25	26	27	28	29	30	31
AUG.	1	2	3	4	5	6	7
	8	9	10	11	12	13	14
	15	16	17	18	19	20	21
	22	23	24	25	26	27	28
	29	30	31				
SEPT.				1	2	3	4
	5	6	7	8	9	10	11
	12	13	14	15	16	17	18
	19	20	21	22	23	24	25
	26	27	28	29	30		
OCT.						1	2
	3	4	5	6	7	8	9
	10	11	12	13	14	15	16
	17	18	19	20	21	22	23
	24	25	26	27	28	29	30
	31						
NOV.		1	2	3	4	5	6
	7	8	9	10	11	12	13
	14	15	16	17	18	19	20
	21	22	23	24	25	26	27
	28	29	30				
DEC.				1	2	3	4
	5	6	7	8	9	10	11
	12	13	14	15	16	17	18
	19	20	21	22	23	24	25
	26	27	28	29	30	31	

1898

	Sunday.	Monday.	Tuesday.	Wednesday.	Thursday.	Friday.	Saturday.
JAN.							1
	2	3	4	5	6	7	8
	9	10	11	12	13	14	15
	16	17	18	19	20	21	22
	23	24	25	26	27	28	29
	30	31					
FEB.			1	2	3	4	5
	6	7	8	9	10	11	12
	13	14	15	16	17	18	19
	20	21	22	23	24	25	26
	27	28					
MAR.			1	2	3	4	5
	6	7	8	9	10	11	12
	13	14	15	16	17	18	19
	20	21	22	23	24	25	26
	27	28	29	30	31		
APRIL						1	2
	3	4	5	6	7	8	9
	10	11	12	13	14	15	16
	17	18	19	20	21	22	23
	24	25	26	27	28	29	30
MAY	1	2	3	4	5	6	7
	8	9	10	11	12	13	14
	15	16	17	18	19	20	21
	22	23	24	25	26	27	28
	29	30	31				
JUNE				1	2	3	4
	5	6	7	8	9	10	11
	12	13	14	15	16	17	18
	19	20	21	22	23	24	25
	26	27	28	29	30		
JULY						1	2
	3	4	5	6	7	8	9
	10	11	12	13	14	15	16
	17	18	19	20	21	22	23
	24	25	26	27	28	29	30
	31						
AUG.		1	2	3	4	5	6
	7	8	9	10	11	12	13
	14	15	16	17	18	19	20
	21	22	23	24	25	26	27
	28	29	30	31			
SEPT.					1	2	3
	4	5	6	7	8	9	10
	11	12	13	14	15	16	17
	18	19	20	21	22	23	24
	25	26	27	28	29	30	
OCT.							1
	2	3	4	5	6	7	8
	9	10	11	12	13	14	15
	16	17	18	19	20	21	22
	23	24	25	26	27	28	29
	30	31					
NOV.			1	2	3	4	5
	6	7	8	9	10	11	12
	13	14	15	16	17	18	19
	20	21	22	23	24	25	26
	27	28	29	30			
DEC.					1	2	3
	4	5	6	7	8	9	10
	11	12	13	14	15	16	17
	18	19	20	21	22	23	24
	25	26	27	28	29	30	31

INDEX.

METHODIST BOOK CONCERN,

EATON & MAINS, 150 Fifth Ave., New York,
CURTS & JENNINGS, 220 W. Fourth St., Cincinnati,

PUBLISH a great variety of Religious Literature, including Bibles, in several sizes and varieties of binding; Commentaries; Church and Sunday School Music; Religious Treatises; Biographies; Hymn Books of the Methodist Episcopal Church, in great varieties of style and sizes; Bible Dictionaries, and the largest collection of Sunday School Literature in the country. German books are published only at Cincinnati, but can be ordered from any of the establishments.

Agents.—All the traveling ministers of the Methodist Episcopal Church who are in full connection are regularly authorized agents of the Methodist Book Concern. Preachers on trial in the Conferences, and local preachers employed to fill vacant appointments, who act as agents for periodicals and purchase of books, are requested to forward the cash with their orders, or, if they wish an account opened, to send a recommendation from the Presiding Elder of the District. A little reflection will show the propriety of this, as the brethren referred to are generally entire strangers to the Book Agents. Presiding Elders will please furnish a list of those they feel willing to recommend at an early period after the session of their Conference.

Our terms to Methodist clergymen are as follows, namely: Discount on books of the **General Catalogue**, including Commentaries, Hymnals, Hymnals with Tunes, and Youths' Library, for cash or ninety days' credit, 30 per cent; for a credit over ninety days, 25 per cent. On Maps, 20 per cent. On Bibles, 20 per cent to 30 per cent. On Epworth Hymnals, for cash, 10 per cent. Cheap and Fifty Volume Libraries in sets, Question Books, Certificates, Class Books, Records, Music Books, Berean Leaves, etc., and books marked thus †, "net."

On Outside Books, from "net" to 30 per cent.

Remit by Draft on New York, Certificate of Deposit, or Post Office Money Order. When these cannot be obtained, send by Registered Letter. Money sent in other ways will be at the sender's risk.

OFFICIAL PERIODICALS.

THE Methodist Book Concern publishes, in its Periodical Department, one Bimonthly, six Quarterlies, two Semimonthlies, three Monthlies, and fourteen Weeklies. Their titles, place of publication, order of issue, terms, and responsible Editors and Publishers are as follows:

Methodist Review, New York, Jan., March, May, July, Sept., Nov...... $2 50
    Wm. V. Kelley, D.D., Editor; Eaton & Mains, Publishers.

Sunday School Journal, New York, Monthly. Single copy.............. 60
    J. L. Hurlbut, D.D., Editor; Eaton & Mains, Publishers.
    In clubs of six and upward, to one address............................. 50

Senior Berean Lesson Quarterly, New York, Quarterly. Per year.. 20
    J. L. Hurlbut, D.D., Editor; Eaton & Mains, Publishers.

Berean Intermediate Lesson Quarterly, N. Y., Quarterly. Per year. 06
    J. L. Hurlbut, D.D., Editor; Eaton & Mains, Publishers.

Berean Beginner's Lesson Quarterly. N. Y., Quarterly. Per year... 06
    J. L. Hurlbut, D.D., Editor; Eaton & Mains, Publishers.

Picture Lesson Paper, New York, Monthly. Per year...................$0 25
    J. L. Hurlbut, D.D., Editor; Eaton & Mains, Publishers.
    In clubs of six and upward, to one address............................. 20
Sunday School Advocate, New York, Weekly. Single copy............ 30
    J. L. Hurlbut, D.D., Editor; Eaton & Mains, Publishers.
    In clubs of six and upward, to one address............................. 25
The Classmate, New York, Biweekly. Single copy...................... 30
    J. L. Hurlbut, D.D., Editor; Eaton & Mains, Publishers.
    In clubs of six and upward, to one address................... 25
Berean Leaf Cluster, New York, Quarterly. Per year................. 4 00
    Eaton & Mains, Publishers.
Berean Lesson Pictures, New York, Quarterly. Per year............. 12
    Eaton & Mains, Publishers.
House and Hearth (German), Cincinnati, Monthly. Per year.......... 2 00
    F. L. Nagler, D.D., Editor; Curts & Jennings, Publishers.
Glocke (German), Cincinnati, Semimonthly. Per year..................... 25
    Curts & Jennings, Publishers.
Bibelforscher (German), Cincinnati, Quarterly. Per year................ 08
    Curts & Jennings, Publishers.
Bildersaal (German), Cincinnati, Quarterly. Per year.................... 4 40
Danneret (Scandinavian), Chicago, Ill.. ....

Weekly Papers.

The Christian Advocate, New York.................................... 2 50
    J. M. Buckley, D.D., Editor; Eaton & Mains, Publishers.
The Epworth Herald, Chicago, Ill. Single copies. 1 00
    Clubs of ten, $10; clubs of twenty-five.................................20 00
    J. F. Berry, D.D., Editor; Curts & Jennings, Publishers.
Western Christian Advocate, Cincinnati, O............................ 2 00
    D. H. Moore, D.D., Editor; Curts & Jennings, Publishers.
Northern Christian Advocate, Syracuse, N. Y.......................... 1 50
    James E. C. Sawyer, D.D., Editor; Eaton & Mains, Publishers.
Northwestern Christian Advocate, Chicago, Ill......................... 2 00
    A. Edwards, D.D., Editor; Curts & Jennings, Publishers.
California Christian Advocate, San Francisco, Cal.................... 2 00
    B. F. Crary, D.D., Editor; Eaton & Mains, Publishers.
Central Christian Advocate, St. Louis, Mo............................ 2 00
    Jesse B. Young, D.D., Editor; Curts & Jennings, Publishers.
Southwestern Christian Advocate, New Orleans, La. 2 00
    I. B. Scott, D.D., Editor; Eaton & Mains, Publishers.
Christian Apologist (German), Cincinnati, O........................... 2 00
    Albert J. Nast, D.D., Editor; Curts & Jennings. Publishers.
Sandebudet; or, Messenger (Scandinavian), Chicago, Ill................. 2 00
    Curts & Jennings, Publishers.
Pittsburg Christian Advocate, Pittsburg, Pa....................... ..... 2 00
    Charles W. Smith, D.D., Editor; Publishers, Conference Committee.
Gevoke (German), Cincinnati,... 50
    Curts & Jennings, Publishers.

REMITTANCES should be made as promptly as possible. Those doing their business with the EASTERN CONCERN should remit by draft on New York; those with the WESTERN, on Cincinnati or Chicago; those on the PACIFIC COAST, on San Francisco.

METHODIST BOOK CONCERN.

NEW YORK: 150 Fifth Ave., EATON & MAINS, Publishing Agents.

DEPOSITORIES:

Boston, Mass., 38 Bromfield Street. Pittsburg, Pa., 524 Penn Avenue.
Buffalo, N. Y., 288 Main Street. San Francisco, 1037 Market Street.
Detroit, Mich., 269 Woodward Avenue.

WESTERN METHODIST BOOK CONCERN.

CINCINNATI:
220 West Fourth Street, CURTS & JENNINGS, Publishing Agents.

DEPOSITORIES:

Chicago, Ill., 57 Washington Street.
St. Louis, Mo., 1505 Locust Street.

All the DEPOSITORIES give the same discounts, credits, etc., to preachers as are given at the principal offices. Payments in San Francisco must be made in gold or its equivalent. Preachers are earnestly desired to make all their credit purchases at one place.

BOOK COMMITTEE.

The Book Committee consists of twenty, chosen by the General Conference, namely:

General Committee by Districts:

DISTRICT I.	S. O. BENTON,	DISTRICT VIII.	O. P. MILLER,
" II.	HENRY SPELLMEYER,	" IX.	S. W. TROUSDALE,
" III.	C. C. WILBOR,	" X.	D. L. RADER,
" IV.	D. S. HAMMOND,	" XI.	HORACE REED,
" V.	W. F. WHITLOCK,	" XII.	HARRY SWANN,
" VI.	J. E. WILSON,	" XIII.	H. A. SALZER,
" VII.	G. O. ROBINSON,	" XIV.	G. M. BOOTH.

Local Committee at New York:

E. B. TUTTLE, J. E. ANDRUS, T. J. PRESTON.

Local Committee at Cincinnati:

RICHARD DYMOND, J. N. GAMBLE, R. T. MILLER.

Friendly Hints to Preachers.—1. In writing to the Agents give your *town, county, State,* and *Conference* distinctly at the top of your sheet.

2. Bear in mind that we do not know your superintendents or other officials, and always indorse their application for grants, or orders for books or periodicals where credit is asked, and have the bill charged to yourself.

BISHOPS.

THOMAS BOWMAN, St. Louis, Mo.; RANDOLPH S. FOSTER, Roxbury, Mass.; STEPHEN M. MERRILL, Chicago, Ill.; EDWARD G. ANDREWS, New York, N.Y.; HENRY W. WARREN, University Park, Colo.; CYRUS D. FOSS, Philadelphia, Pa.; JOHN F. HURST, Washington, D. C.; WILLIAM X. NINDE, Detroit, Mich.; JOHN M. WALDEN, Cincinnati, O.; WILLARD F. MALLALIEU, Boston, Mass.; CHARLES H. FOWLER, Buffalo, N. Y.; JOHN H. VINCENT, Topeka, Kan.; JAMES N. FITZGERALD, St. Louis, Mo.; ISAAC W. JOYCE, Minneapolis, Minn.; JOHN P. NEWMAN, San Francisco, Cal.; DANIEL A. GOODSELL, Chattanooga, Tenn.; CHARLES C. MCCABE, Fort Worth, Tex.; EARL CRANSTON, Portland, Ore.; WILLIAM TAYLOR, New York, N. Y.; JAMES M. THOBURN, Bombay, India; JOSEPH C. HARTZELL, Vivi, Congo, Africa.

TRUSTEES.

OFFICE, Cincinnati, O.—*President*, JOHN M. WALDEN; *Secretary*, JOHN PEARSON; *Treasurer*, GEORGE B. JOHNSON.

TERM EXPIRES IN 1900.—*Ministers:* LUKE HITCHCOCK, EARL CRANSTON, JOHN PEARSON. *Laymen:* JAMES N. GAMBLE, GEORGE B. JOHNSON, WILLIAM NEWKIRK.

TERM EXPIRES IN 1904.—*Ministers:* JOHN M. WALDEN, LEWIS CURTS, DAVID H. MOORE. *Laymen:* ROBERT T. MILLER, JOHN D. HEARNE, WILLIAM F. BOYD.

The Trustees are elected by and are amenable to the General Conference. The Board has power to receive, hold, and administer on any property by gift, devise, or otherwise confided to it, in behoof of and for the benefit of the Methodist Episcopal Church. It is also competent to receive and administer on any special benevolent trust not otherwise provided for in the other benevolent societies of the Methodist Episcopal Church.

MISSIONARY SOCIETY.

OFFICE, 150 Fifth Avenue, New York.—Bishop S. M. MERRILL, *President*; A. B. LEONARD, D.D., A. J. PALMER, D.D., W. T. SMITH, D.D., *Corresponding Secretaries*; HOMER EATON, D.D., *Treasurer*; LEWIS CURTS, D.D., *Assistant Treasurer*, Cincinnati, O.; S. L. BALDWIN, D.D., *Recording Secretary*.

Members of General Committees on Missions, Church Extension, and Freedmen's Aid and Southern Education.

This Committee is composed of the Board of Bishops, the Secretaries and Treasurers of the Missionary Society, fourteen members appointed by the Board of Managers, and a like number appointed by the General Conference. The members appointed by the General Conference hold office for four years, or until the ensuing General Conference. Those representing the Managers are appointed annually. The Committee appointed by the General Conference for 1896–1900 consists of:

DISTRICT		DISTRICT	
I.	E. M. SMITH,	VIII.	H. G. JACKSON,
II.	MERRITT HULBURD,	IX.	J. F. CHAFFEE,
III.	D. F. PIERCE,	X.	ALFRED HODGETTS,
IV.	R. T. MILLER,	XI.	W. J. MARTINDALE,
V.	L. H. STEWART,	XII.	A. J. TAYLOR,
VI.	J. M. CARTER,	XIII.	BARTHOLOMEW LAMPERT,
VII.	H. N. HERRICK,	XIV.	S. A. THOMSON.

SUNDAY SCHOOL UNION.

OFFICE, 150 Fifth Avenue, New York.—S. M. MERRILL, *President*; T. Y. KINNE, *Vice President*; J. L. HURLBUT, D.D., *Corresponding Secretary*; F. L. NAGLER, D.D., *German Assistant Secretary*; R. R. DOHERTY, *Recording Secretary*; D. DENHAM, *Treasurer*.

All communications respecting statistics and the general business of the Sunday School Union of the Methodist Episcopal Church should be addressed to the *Corresponding Secretary*, J. L. HURLBUT, D.D., 150 Fifth Avenue, New York.

Funds may be remitted to the *Treasurer*, DANIEL DENHAM, at the same place.

Remittances may also be made to any one of the treasurers of the various *local committees*, as follows: George B. Johnson, 220 West Fourth Street, Cincinnati, O.; C. R. Magee, 38 Bromfield Street, Boston, Mass.; O. A. Oliver, 57 Washington Street, Chicago, Ill.; W. M. Swindells, D.D., 1018 Arch Street, Philadelphia, Pa.; J. Lanahan, D.D., 118 East Baltimore Street, Baltimore, Md.; S. H. Pye, 1505 Locust Street, St. Louis, Mo.; William Abbott, 1037 Market Street, San Francisco, Cal.; J. E. Mason, 269 Woodward Avenue, Detroit, Mich.; J. Horner, D.D., 524 Penn Avenue, Pittsburg, Pa.

Applications for aid in behalf of Sunday schools should be addressed to the Corresponding Secretary at New York, or to the secretary of the local committee nearest to the applicant, thereby saving in cost of transportation. The persons above named as treasurers of the local committees are also secretaries of the same.

No application can be considered unless the school for which aid is asked is connected with the Methodist Episcopal Church.

The Pastor or Presiding Elder must further certify that, in his judgment, the school is *needy*, as it is not the design of the Union to afford aid to schools that are able to sustain themselves.

TRACT SOCIETY.

OFFICE, 150 Fifth Avenue, New York.—S. M. MERRILL, *President;* RICHARD LAVERY, *Vice President;* J. L. HURLBUT, D.D., *Corresponding Secretary;* F. L. NAGLER, D.D., *German Assistant Secretary;* JAMES M. FREEMAN, D.D., *Recording Secretary;* GEORGE P. MAINS, D.D., *Treasurer.*

All communications respecting the general business of the Society should be addressed to the *Corresponding Secretary,* J. L. HURLBUT, D.D., 150 Fifth Avenue, New York.

Funds may be remitted to the *Treasurer,* GEORGE P. MAINS, D.D., at the same place.

Remittances may also be made to any one of the treasurers of the various *local committees,* as follows: George B. Johnson, 220 West Fourth Street, Cincinnati, O.; C. R. Magee, 38 Bromfield Street, Boston, Mass.; O. A. Oliver, 57 Washington Street, Chicago, Ill.; W. M. Swindells, D.D., 1018 Arch Street, Philadelphia, Pa.; J. Lanahan, D.D., 118 East Baltimore Street, Baltimore, Md.; S. H. Pye, 1505 Locust Street, St. Louis, Mo.; William Abbott, 1037 Market Street, San Francisco, Cal.; J. Horner, D.D., 524 Penn Avenue, Pittsburg, Pa.; J. E. Mason, 269 Woodward Avenue, Detroit, Mich.

Applications for grants should be addressed to the Corresponding Secretary at New York, or to the Secretary of the local committee nearest to the applicant. The persons above named as treasurers of the local committees are also secretaries of the same.

BOARD OF CHURCH EXTENSION.

OFFICE, 1026 Arch Street, Philadelphia. — Bishop C. D. FOSS, *President;* A. J. KYNETT, D.D., and W. A. SPENCER, *Corresponding Secretaries;* JAMES LONG, *Treasurer;* MANLEY S. HARD, *Assistant Corresponding Secretary.* For list of General Committee see page 8.

Organization.—This Society was organized by direction of the General Conference of 1864, and was incorporated by the Legislature of Pennsylvania, March 13, 1865. On recommendation of the Board of Managers the Constitution was revised and more closely identified with the economy of the Church by the General Conference of 1872, which also inserted an important section in relation to the Society in the Discipline of the Church.

BOARD OF EDUCATION.

DIRECTORY AND EXPLANATIONS.

CORPORATE NAME: The Board of Education of the Methodist Episcopal Church.

OFFICE, 150 Fifth Avenue (corner of 20th Street), **New York.**

The Annual Meeting of the Board is held in New York the First Wednesday in December.

Officers: *President,* Bishop E. G. ANDREWS, D.D.; *Recording Secretary,* A. S. HUNT, D.D.; *Treasurer,* JOSEPH S. STOUT; *Corresponding Secretary,* C. H. PAYNE, D.D.

The Corresponding Secretary has charge of the general correspondence and executive business of the Board. Collections and returned loans are sent to him. His official address is 150 Fifth Avenue, New York.

The Treasurer, JOSEPH S. STOUT, receives from the Corresponding Secretary and the several Book Agents all remittances, and holds all funds of the Board, and makes all disbursements on the Secretary's order.

N. B.—As the Treasurer's countinghouse is in another part of the city, it is for his convenience to have the details of accounts kept at the office of the Corresponding Secretary.

Committees: Apportionments to the several institutions of learning are made annually by the Apportionment Committee. The Finance Committee has supervision of the expenses and of the finances in general, and the Auditing Committee examines the Treasurer's accounts.

For the Term to Expire in 1900.—Bishop E. G. ANDREWS, GEORGE P. HUKELL, ALBERT S. HUNT, JAMES LONG.

For the Term to Expire in 1904.—JOHN W. LINDSAY, MARK HOYT, LEWIS R. FISKE, JOSEPH S. STOUT.

For the Term to Expire in 1908.—Bishop JOHN F. HURST, OLIVER H. DURRELL, WILLIAM F. KING, JOHN D. SLAYBACK.

FREEDMEN'S AID AND SOUTHERN EDUCATION SOCIETY.

OFFICE, Cincinnati, O.—Bishop J. M. WALDEN, D.D., *President;* R. S. RUST, *Honorary Secretary;* JOHN W. HAMILTON and MADISON C. B. MASON, *Corresponding Secretaries;* WILLIAM H. H. REES, *Recording Secretary;* LEWIS CURTS, *Treasurer;* HOMER EATON, *Assistant Treasurer.*

For list of General Committee see page 8.

The Society was organized in November, 1866, its object being to promote the mental and religious improvement of the freedmen of the South. During the ensuing seven years it received and expended over $430,000.

WOMAN'S FOREIGN MISSIONARY SOCIETY.

Officers: *General Secretary,* Mrs. J. T. GRACEY; *Treasurer,* Mrs. WILLIAM B. SKIDMORE.

Committee on References: *Chairman,* Mrs. W. B. SKIDMORE, No. 230 West 59th Street, New York city; *Secretary,* Mrs. B. R. COWAN, No. 7 Crescent Place, Walnut Hills, Cincinnati, O.

Woman's Missionary Friend: *Agent,* Miss P. J. WALDEN, No. 36 Bromfield Street, Boston, Mass.; *Editor,* Miss LOUISE MANNING HODGKINS, Auburndale, Mass.

WOMAN'S HOME MISSIONARY SOCIETY.

President, Mrs. CLINTON B. FISK, 175 West 58th Street, New York city; *Vice Presidents,* Mrs. F. S. HOYT, Mrs. H. C. MCCABE, Mrs. Bishop WALDEN, Mrs. J. B. ROBINSON, Mrs. W. G. WILLIAMS; *Corresponding Secretary,* Mrs. R. S. RUST, No. 623 West Fourth Street, Cincinnati, O.; *Treasurer,* Mrs. J. W. MENDENHALL, Delaware, O.; *Recording Secretary,* Mrs. F. A. AIKEN, No. 15 Grand Street, Walnut Hills, Cincinnati, O.

Woman's Home Missions: *Editor,* Mrs. H. C. MCCABE; *Publisher,* Miss M. B. EVANS, Delaware, O.

EPWORTH LEAGUE.

OFFICE, 57 Washington Street, Chicago, Ill.—*General Secretary,* EDWIN A. SCHELL.

Board of Control.—1. Appointed by the Bishops: Bishop W. X. NINDE, *President;* W. I. HAVEN, J. H. COLEMAN, E. M. MILLS, J. W. E. BOWEN, S. O. ROYAL, J. A. PATTEN, F. A. CHAMBERLAIN, R. R. DOHERTY, W. L. WOODCOCK, R. S. COPELAND, H. A. SCHROETTER, C. E. PIPER, F. D. FULLER, L. J. NORTON.

2. Elected by the General Conference:

DISTRICT		DISTRICT	
I.	C. R. MAGEE,	VIII.	J. B. ALBROOK,
II.	E. S. OSBON,	IX.	W. H. JORDAN,
III.	S. A. MORSE,	X.	B. L. PAINE,
IV.	F. W. TUNNELL,	XI.	J. W. VAN CLEVE,
V.	B. E. HELMAN,	XII.	FRANK GARY,
VI.	M. M. ALSTON,	XIII.	WILLIAM KOENEKE,
VII.	W. D. PARR,	XIV.	J. W. BENNETT.

BOARD OF INSURANCE.

Appointed by the Board of Bishops: J. B. HOBBS, A. B. BURKE, J. R. LINDGREN, G. B. JOHNSON, and N. W. HARRIS.

Elected by the General Conference:

DISTRICT		DISTRICT	
I.	H. H. SHAW,	VIII.	C. E. LANE,
II.	C. D. HAMMOND,	IX.	H. P. MAGILL,
III.	J. E. BILLS,	X.	T. L. MATHEWS
IV.	W. M. SWINDELLS,	XI.	T. J. GREEN,
V.	F. H. TANNER,	XII.	E. H. MCKISSACK,
VI.	J. S. HILL,	XIII.	C. E. MUELLER,
VII.	A. M. GOULD,	XIV.	J. D. HAMMOND.

THE MINISTRATION OF BAPTISM TO INFANTS.

The Minister, coming to the Font, which is to be filled with pure Water, shall use the following :

DEARLY BELOVED : Forasmuch as all men are conceived and born in sin, and that our Saviour Christ saith, Except a man be born of water and of the Spirit he cannot enter into the kingdom of God ; I beseech you to call upon God the Father, through our Lord Jesus Christ, that having, of his bounteous mercy, redeemed *this child* by the blood of his Son, he will grant that *he,* being baptized with water, may also be baptized with the Holy Ghost, be received into Christ's holy Church, and become *a lively member* of the same.

Then shall the Minister say,

Let us pray.

Almighty and everlasting God, who of thy great mercy hast condescended to enter into covenant relations with man, wherein thou hast included children as partakers of its gracious benefits, declaring that of such is thy kingdom : and in thy ancient Church didst appoint divers baptisms, figuring thereby the renewing of the Holy Ghost ; and by thy well-beloved Son Jesus Christ gavest commandment to thy holy Apostles to go into all the world and disciple all nations, baptizing them in the name of the Father, and of the Son, and of the Holy Ghost : We beseech thee, that of thine infinite mercy thou wilt look upon *this child :* wash *him* and sanctify *him ;* that *he,* being saved by thy grace, may be received into Christ's holy Church, and being steadfast in faith, joyful through hope, and rooted in love, may so overcome the evils of this present world, that finally *he* may attain to everlasting life, and reign with thee, world without end, through Jesus Christ our Lord. *Amen.*

O merciful God, grant that all carnal affections may die in *him*, and that all things belonging to the Spirit may live and grow in *him*. *Amen.*

Grant that *he* may have power and strength to have victory, and to triumph against the devil, the world, and the flesh. *Amen.*

Grant that whosoever is dedicated to thee by our office and ministry may also be endued with heavenly virtues, and everlastingly rewarded through thy mercy, O blessed Lord God, who dost live, and govern all things, world without end. *Amen.*

Almighty, ever-living God, whose most dearly beloved Son Jesus Christ, for the forgiveness of our sins, did shed out of his most precious side both water and blood, regard, we beseech thee, our supplications. Sanctify this water for this holy sacrament; and grant that *this child*, now to be baptized, may receive the fullness of thy grace, and ever remain in the number of thy faithful and elect children, through Jesus Christ our Lord. *Amen.*

Then shall the Minister address the Parents [or Guardians]
as follows :

Dearly beloved : Forasmuch as *this child is* now presented by you for Christian baptism, *you* must remember that it is your part and duty to see that *he* be taught, as soon as *he* shall be able to learn, the nature and end of this holy sacrament. And that *he* may know these things the better, *you* shall call upon *him* to give reverent attendance upon the appointed means of grace, such as the ministry of the word and the public and private worship of God ; and further, ye shall provide that *he* shall read the Holy Scriptures, and learn the Lord's Prayer, the Ten Commandments, the Apostles' Creed, the Catechism, and all other things which a Christian ought to know and believe to *his* soul's health, in order

that *he* may be brought up to lead a virtuous and holy
life, remembering always that baptism doth represent
unto us that inward purity which disposeth us to follow
the example of our Saviour Christ; that as he died and
rose again for us, so should we, who are baptized, die
unto sin and rise again unto righteousness, continually
mortifying all corrupt affections, and daily proceeding
in all virtue and godliness.

Do *you* therefore solemnly engage to fulfill these du-
ties, so far as in you lies, the Lord being your helper?
Ans. We do.

Then shall the people stand up, and the Minister shall say:

Hear the words of the Gospel, written by St. Mark.
[Chap. x, 13–16.]

They brought young children to Christ, that he should
touch them. And his disciples rebuked those that
brought them. But when Jesus saw it, he was much
displeased, and said unto them, Suffer the little children
to come unto me, and forbid them not, for of such is the
kingdom of God. Verily I say unto you, whosoever
shall not receive the kingdom of God as a little child,
he shall not enter therein. And he took them up in
his arms, put his hands upon them, and blessed them.

*Then the Minister shall take the Child into his hands, and
say to the friends of the Child,*

Name this child.

*And then, naming it after them, he shall sprinkle or pour
Water upon it, or, if desired, immerse it in Water, saying,*

N., I baptize thee in the name of the Father, and of
the Son, and of the Holy Ghost. *Amen.*

*Then shall the Minister offer the following prayer, the people
kneeling :*

O God of infinite mercy, the Father of all the faithful
seed, be pleased to grant unto this child an understand-

ing mind and a sanctified heart. May thy providence lead *him* through the dangers, temptations, and ignorance of *his* youth, that *he* may never run into folly nor into the evils of an unbridled appetite. We pray thee so to order the course of *his* life, that by good education, by holy examples, and by thy restraining and renewing grace, *he* may be led to serve thee faithfully all *his* days, so that, when *he* has glorified thee in *his* generation, and has served the Church on earth, *he* may be received into thine eternal kingdom, through Jesus Christ our Lord. *Amen.*

Almighty and most merciful Father, let thy loving mercy and compassion descend upon these, thy servant and handmaid, the parents [or guardians] of this child. Grant unto them, we beseech thee, thy Holy Spirit, that they may, like Abraham, command their household to keep the way of the Lord. Direct their actions and sanctify their hearts, words, and purposes, that their whole family may be united to our Lord Jesus Christ in the bands of faith, obedience, and charity ; and that they all, being in this life thy holy children by adoption and grace, may be admitted into the Church of the first-born in heaven, through the merits of thy dear Son, our Saviour and Redeemer. *Amen.*

Then may the Minister offer extemporary prayer.

Then shall be said, all kneeling :

Our Father who art in heaven, hallowed be thy name. Thy kingdom come. Thy will be done in earth as it is in heaven. Give us this day our daily bread ; and forgive us our trespasses as we forgive them that trespass against us ; and lead us not into temptation, but deliver us from evil; for thine is the kingdom, and the power, and the glory, forever. *Amen.*

FORM
FOR THE SOLEMNIZATION OF MATRIMONY.

[The parts in brackets throughout may be used or not, at discretion.]

At the day and time appointed for Solemnization of Matrimony, the persons to be married—having been qualified according to law—standing together, the Man on the right hand, and the Woman on the left, the Minister shall say:

DEARLY BELOVED: We are gathered together here in the sight of God, and in the presence of these witnesses, to join together this man and this woman in holy matrimony ; which is an honorable estate, instituted of God in the time of man's innocency, signifying unto us the mystical union that is between Christ and his Church; which holy estate Christ adorned and beautified with his presence, and first miracle that he wrought, in Cana of Galilee, and is commended of St. Paul to be honorable among all men ; and therefore is not by any to be entered into unadvisedly, but reverently, discreetly, and in the fear of God.

Into which holy estate these two persons present come now to be joined. Therefore if any can show just cause why they may not lawfully be joined together, let him now speak, or else hereafter forever hold his peace.

[And also speaking unto the persons that are to be married, the Minister shall say:

I require and charge you both, that if either of you know any impediment why you may not be lawfully joined together in matrimony, you do now confess it; for be ye well assured, that so many as are coupled together otherwise than God's word doth allow, are not joined together by God, neither is their matrimony lawful.]

If no impediment be alleged, then shall the Minister say unto the Man,

M., wilt thou have this woman to be thy wedded wife, to live together after God's ordinance in the holy estate of matrimony? Wilt thou love her, comfort her, honor, and keep her, in sickness and in health : and forsaking all other, keep thee only unto her, so long as ye both shall live?

The Man shall answer,

I will.

Then shall the Minister say unto the Woman,

N., wilt thou have this man to be thy wedded husband, to live together after God's ordinance in the holy estate of matrimony? Wilt thou love, honor, and keep him, in sickness and in health : and forsaking all other, keep thee only unto him, so long as ye both shall live?

The Woman shall answer,

I will.

[*Then the Minister shall cause the Man with his right hand to take the Woman by her right hand, and to say after him as followeth:*

I, *M.*, take thee, *N.*, to be my wedded wife, to have and to hold, from this day forward, for better, for worse, for richer, for poorer, in sickness and in health, to love and to cherish, till death us do part, according to God's holy ordinance : and thereto I plight thee my faith.

Then shall they loose their hands, and the Woman with her right hand taking the Man by his right hand, shall likewise say after the Minister:

I, *N.*, take thee, *M.*, to be my wedded husband, to have and to hold, from this day forward, for better, for worse, for richer, for poorer, in sickness and in health, to love and to cherish, till death us do part, according to God's holy ordinance ; and thereto I plight thee my faith.]

Then shall the Minister pray thus:

O Eternal God, Creator and Preserver of all mankind, Giver of all spiritual grace, the Author of everlasting life ; send thy blessing upon these thy servants, this man and this woman ; whom we bless in thy name; that as Isaac and Rebecca lived faithfully together, so these persons may surely perform and keep the vow and covenant between them made, and may ever remain in perfect love and peace together, and live according to thy laws, through Jesus Christ our Lord. *Amen.*

[*If the parties desire it, the Man shall here hand a ring to the Minister, who shall return it to him, and direct him to place it on the third finger of the Woman's left hand. And the man shall say to the woman, repeating after the Minister :*

With this ring I thee wed, and with my worldly goods I thee endow, in the name of the Father, and of the Son, and of the Holy Ghost. *Amen.*]

Then shall the Minister join their right hands together, and say :

Forasmuch as *M.* and *N.* have consented together in holy wedlock, and have witnessed the same before God and this company, and thereto have pledged their faith either to other, and have declared the same by joining of hands; I pronounce that they are husband and wife together, in the name of the Father, and of the Son, and of the Holy Ghost. Those whom God hath joined together, let no man put asunder. *Amen.*

And the Minister shall add this blessing :

God, the Father, the Son, and the Holy Ghost, bless, preserve, and keep you; the Lord mercifully with his

favor look upon you, and so fill you with all spiritual
benediction and grace, that ye may so live together in
this life, that in the world to come ye may have life
everlasting. *Amen.*

Then shall the Minister offer the following Prayer:

O God of Abraham, God of Isaac, God of Jacob,
bless this man and this woman, and sow the seed of
eternal life in their hearts, that whatsoever in thy holy
word they shall profitably learn, they may indeed fulfill
the same.   Look, O Lord, mercifully on them from
heaven, and bless them : as thou didst send thy blessings upon Abraham and Sarah, to their great comfort,
so vouchsafe to send thy blessings upon this man and
this woman, that they, obeying thy will, and always being in safety under thy protection, may abide in thy
love unto their lives' end, through Jesus Christ our
Lord.

Almighty God, who at the beginning didst create our
first parents, Adam and Eve, and didst sanctify and join
them together in marriage, pour upon these persons the
riches of thy grace, sanctify and bless them, that they
may please thee both in body and soul, and live together in holy love unto their lives' end. *Amen.*

Here the Minister may use extemporary Prayer.

Then the Minister shall repeat the Lord's Prayer:

Our Father who art in heaven, hallowed be thy name.
Thy kingdom come.   Thy will be done in earth as it is
in heaven.   Give us this day our daily bread; and forgive us our trespasses, as we forgive them that trespass
against us ; and lead us not into temptation, but deliver
us from evil ; for thine is the kingdom, and the power,
and the glory, forever. *Amen.*

VISITING THE SICK.

SCRIPTURE LESSONS.

GROUNDS FOR HOPE.

FOR God sent not his Son into the world to condemn the world ; but that the world through him might be saved. [John iii, 17.]

The Lord is not slack concerning his promise, as some men count slackness ; but is long-suffering to us-ward, not willing that any should perish, but that all should come to repentance. [2 Pet. iii, 9.]

Therefore, O thou son of man, speak unto the house of Israel ; Thus ye speak, saying, If our transgressions and our sins be upon us, and we pine away in them, how should we then live ? Say unto them, As I live, saith the Lord GOD, I have no pleasure in the death of the wicked ; but that the wicked turn from his way and live : turn ye, turn ye from your evil ways ; for why will ye die, O house of Israel ? [Ezek. xxxiii, 10, 11.]

He that spared not his own Son, but delivered him up for us all, how shall he not with him also freely give us all things ? [Rom. viii, 32.]

But we see Jesus, who was made a little lower than the angels for the suffering of death, crowned with glory and honor ; that he by the grace of God should taste death for every man. [Heb. ii, 9.]

Come unto me, all ye that labor and are heavy laden, and I will give you rest. Take my yoke upon you, and learn of me ; for I am meek and lowly in heart : and ye shall find rest unto your souls. [Matt. xi, 28, 29.]

Look unto me, and be ye saved, all the ends of the earth : for I am God, and there is none else. [Isa. xlv, 22.]

And the Spirit and the bride say, Come. And let

him that heareth say, Come. And let him that is athirst come. And whosoever will, let him take the water of life freely. [Rev. xxii, 17.]

Him that cometh to me I will in no wise cast out. [John vi, 37.]

He that covereth his sins shall not prosper : but whoso confesseth and forsaketh them shall have mercy. [Prov. xxviii, 13.]

TERMS OF SALVATION.

If thou shalt confess with thy mouth the Lord Jesus, and shalt believe in thine heart that God hath raised him from the dead, thou shalt be saved. For with the heart man believeth unto righteousness, and with the mouth confession is made unto salvation. For the Scripture saith, Whosoever believeth on him shall not be ashamed. For there is no difference between the Jew and the Greek : for the same Lord over all is rich unto all that call upon him. For whosoever shall call upon the name of the Lord shall be saved. [Rom. x, 9-13.]

Not by works of righteousness which we have done, but according to his mercy he saved us, by the washing of regeneration, and renewing of the Holy Ghost. [Titus iii, 5.]

He that believeth and is baptized shall be saved ; but he that believeth not shall be damned. [Mark xvi, 16.]

And as Moses lifted up the serpent in the wilderness, even so must the Son of man be lifted up : that whosoever believeth in him should not perish, but have eternal life. For God so loved the world, that he gave his only begotten Son, that whosoever believeth in him should not perish, but have everlasting life. [John iii, 14-16.]

Behold, happy is the man whom God correcteth : therefore despise not thou the chastening of the Almighty. [Job v, 17.]

For whom the Lord loveth he correcteth; even as a father the son in whom he delighteth. [Prov. iii, 12.]

I know, O Lord, that thy judgments are right, and that thou in faithfulness hast afflicted me. [Psa. cxix, 75.]

Thou shalt also consider in thine heart, that, as a man chasteneth his son, so the Lord thy God chasteneth thee. [Deut. viii, 5.]

Blessed are they that mourn : for they shall be comforted. [Matt. v, 4.]

For our light affliction, which is but for a moment, worketh for us a far more exceeding and eternal weight of glory ; while we look not at the things which are seen, but at the things which are not seen. [2 Cor. iv, 17, 18.]

Beloved, think it not strange concerning the fiery trial which is to try you, as though some strange thing happened unto you : but rejoice, inasmuch as ye are partakers of Christ's sufferings ; that, when his glory shall be revealed, ye may be glad also with exceeding joy. [1 Pet. iv, 12, 13.]

For the Lord will not cast off forever : but though he cause grief, yet will he have compassion according to the multitude of his mercies. For he doth not afflict willingly, nor grieve the children of men. [Lam. iii, 31–33.]

It is good for me that I have been afflicted ; that I might learn thy statutes. [Psa. cxix, 71.]

Before I was afflicted I went astray: but now have I kept thy word. [Psa. cxix, 67.]

Fear thou not; for I am with thee : be not dismayed; for I am thy God : I will strengthen thee; yea, I will help thee ; yea, I will uphold thee with the right hand of my righteousness. [Isa. xli, 10.]

Precious in the sight of the Lord is the death of his saints. [Psa. cxvi, 15.]

He hath said, I will never leave thee, nor forsake thee. [Heb. xiii, 5.]

Cast thy burden upon the Lord, and he shall sustain thee. [Psa. lv, 22.]

Yea, though I walk through the valley of the shadow of death, I will fear no evil: for thou art with me; thy rod and thy staff they comfort me. [Psa. xxiii, 4.]

Thou will keep him in perfect peace whose mind is stayed on thee : because he trusteth in thee. [Isa. xxvi, 3.]

And the Lord, he it is that doth go before thee; he will be with thee, he will not fail thee, neither forsake thee : fear not, neither be dismayed. [Deut. xxxi, 8.]

And I heard a voice from heaven saying unto me, Write, Blessed are the dead which die in the Lord from henceforth : Yea, saith the Spirit, that they may rest from their labors, and their works do follow them. [Rev. xiv, 13.]

Marvel not at this : for the hour is coming, in the which all that are in the graves shall hear his voice, and shall come forth : they that have done good, unto the resurrection of life; and they that have done evil, unto the resurrection of damnation. [John v, 28, 29.]

Jesus said unto her, I am the resurrection, and the life : he that believeth in me, though he were dead, yet shall he live : and whosoever liveth and believeth in me shall never die. [John xi, 25, 26.]

Mark the perfect man, and behold the upright: for the end of that man is peace. [Psa. xxxvii, 37.]

My flesh and my heart faileth : but God is the strength of my heart, and my portion forever. [Psa. lxxiii, 26.]

The wicked is driven away in his wickedness : but the righteous hath hope in his death. [Prov. xiv, 32.]

For whether we live, we live unto the Lord; and whether we die, we die unto the Lord: whether we live therefore, or die, we are the Lord's. [Rom. xiv, 8.]

O death, where is thy sting? O grave, where is thy victory? . . . Thanks be to God, which giveth us the victory through our Lord Jesus Christ. [1 Cor. xv, 55, 57.]

I know whom I have believed, and am persuaded that he is able to keep that which I have committed unto him against that day. [2 Tim. i, 12.]

As the children are partakers of flesh and blood, he also himself likewise took part of the same; that through death he might . . . deliver them, who through fear of death were all their life-time subject to bondage. [Heb. ii, 14, 15.]

O death, I will be thy plagues; O grave, I will be thy destruction. [Hos. xiii, 14.]

He will swallow up death in victory. [Isa. xxv, 8.]

Let me die the death of the righteous, and let my last end be like his. [Num. xxiii, 10.]

And God shall wipe away all tears from their eyes; and there shall be no more death, neither sorrow, nor crying, neither shall there be any more pain: for the former things have passed away. [Rev. xxi, 4.]

And there shall be no night there ; and they need no candle, neither light of the sun; for the Lord God giveth them light, and they shall reign for ever and ever. [Rev. xxii, 5.]

FUNERAL OF A CHRISTIAN.

SCRIPTURE LESSONS.

IS there not an appointed time to man upon earth? are not his days also like the days of a hireling? [Job vii, 1.]

When a few years are come, then I shall go the way whence I shall not return. [Job xvi, 22.]

For I know that thou wilt bring me to death, and to the house appointed for all living. [Job xxx, 23.]

Mark the perfect man, and behold the upright: for the end of that man is peace. [Psa. xxxvii, 37.]

Precious in the sight of the Lord is the death of his saints. [Psa. cxvi, 15.]

For to me to live is Christ, and to die is gain. [Phil. i, 21.]

For I am in a strait betwixt two, having a desire to depart, and to be with Christ; which is far better. [Phil. i, 23.]

I would not live always. [Job vii, 16.]

Yea, though I walk through the valley of the shadow of death, I will fear no evil: for thou art with me; thy rod and thy staff they comfort me. [Psa. xxiii, 4.]

There the wicked cease from troubling; and there the weary be at rest. [Job. iii, 17.]

If a man die, shall he live again? [Job xiv, 14.]

For I know that my Redeemer liveth, and that he shall stand at the latter day upon the earth. [Job xix, 25.]

Now that the dead are raised, even Moses showed at the bush, when he calleth the Lord the God of Abraham, and the God of Isaac, and the God of Jacob. [Luke xx, 37.]

For this corruptible must put on incorruption, and this mortal must put on immortality. [1 Cor. xv, 53.]

Jesus said unto her, I am the resurrection, and the

life: he that believeth in me, though he were dead, yet shall he live. [John xi, 25.]

So when this corruptible shall have put on incorruption, and this mortal shall have put on immortality, then shall be brought to pass the saying that is written, Death is swallowed up in victory. [1 Cor. xv, 54.]

For we know that, if our earthly house of this tabernacle were dissolved, we have a building of God, a house not made with hands, eternal in the heavens. [2 Cor. v, 7.]

And God shall wipe away all tears from their eyes; and there shall be no more death, neither sorrow, nor crying, neither shall there be any more pain: for the former things are passed away. [Rev. xxi, 4.]

And there shall be no night there; and they need no candle, neither light of the sun; for the Lord God giveth them light: and they shall reign for ever and ever. [Rev. xxii, 5.]

And though after my skin worms destroy this body, yet in my flesh shall I see God. Whom I shall see for myself, and mine eyes shall behold, and not another; though my reins be consumed within me. [Job xix, 26, 27.]

For he is not a God of the dead, but of the living. [Luke xx, 38.]

And whosoever liveth, and believeth in me, shall never die. [John xi, 26.]

O death, where is thy sting? O grave, where is thy victory? The sting of death is sin; and the strength of sin is the law. But thanks be to God, which giveth us the victory, through our Lord Jesus Christ. [1 Cor. xv, 55–57.]

We are confident, I say, and willing rather to be absent from the body, and to be present with the Lord [2 Cor. v, 8.]

FUNERAL OF AN UNCONVERTED PERSON.

SCRIPTURE LESSONS.

WHEREFORE, as by one man sin entered into the world, and death by sin; and so death passed upon all men, for that all have sinned. [Rom. v, 12.]

What man is he that liveth, and shall not see death? shall he deliver his soul from the hand of the grave? [Psa. lxxxix, 48.]

For dust thou art, and unto dust shalt thou return. [Gen. iii, 19.]

Your fathers, where are they? and the prophets, do they live forever? [Zech. i, 5.]

When a few years are come, then I shall go the way whence I shall not return. [Job. xvi, 22.]

For I know that thou wilt bring me to death, and to the house appointed for all living. [Job xxx, 23.]

.There is no man that hath power over the spirit to retain the spirit; neither hath he power in the day of death: and there is no discharge in that war; neither shall wickedness deliver those that are given to it. [Eccl. viii, 8.]

The days of our years are threescore years and ten; and if by reason of strength they be fourscore years, yet is their strength labor and sorrow; for it is soon cut off, and we fly away. [Psa. xc, 10.]

For he knoweth our frame; he remembereth that we are dust. As for man, his days are as grass: as a flower of the field, so he flourisheth. For the wind passeth over it, and it is gone; and the place thereof shall know it no more. [Psa. ciii, 14–16.]

Man that is born of a woman is of few days, and full of trouble. He cometh forth like a flower, and is cut down: he fleeth also as a shadow, and continueth not [Job xiv, 1, 2.]

Then shall the dust return to the ·earth as it was : and the spirit shall return unto God who gave it. [Eccl. xii, 7.]

Watch therefore ; for ye know neither the day nor the hour wherein the Son of man cometh. [Matt. xxv, 13.]

Whatsoever thy hand findeth to do, do it with thy might ; for there is no work, nor device, nor knowledge, nor wisdom, in the grave, whither thou goest. [Eccl. ix, 10.]

Let your loins be girded about, and your lights burning ; and ye yourselves like unto men that wait for their lord, when he will return from the wedding ; that, when he cometh and knocketh, they may open unto him immediately. Blessed are those servants, whom the lord when he cometh shall find watching. [Luke xii, 35–37.]

For we must all appear before the judgment-seat of Christ. [2 Cor. v, 10.]

FUNERAL OF AN INFANT.

SCRIPTURE LESSONS.

BUT when David saw that his servants whispered, David perceived that the child was dead : therefore David said unto his servants, Is the child dead ? And they said, He is dead. [2 Sam. xii, 19.]

Then said his servants unto him, What thing is this that thou hast done ? thou didst fast and weep for the child, while it was alive ; but when the child was dead, thou didst rise and eat bread. And he said, While the child was yet alive, I fasted, and wept : for I said, Who can tell whether God will be gracious to me, that the child may live ? But now he is dead, wherefore should

I fast? can I bring him back again? I shall go to him, but he shall not return to me. [2 Sam. xii, 21-23.]

And they brought young children to him, that he should touch them; and his disciples rebuked those that brought them. But when Jesus saw it, he was much displeased, and said unto them, Suffer the little children to come unto me, and forbid them not; for of such is the kingdom of God. Verily I say unto you, Whosoever shall not receive the kingdom of God as a little child, he shall not enter therein. And he took them up in his arms, put his hands upon them, and blessed them. [Mark x, 13-16.]

And he took a child, and set him in the midst of them: and when he had taken him in his arms, he said unto them, Whosoever shall receive one of such chlidren in my name, receiveth me; and whosoever shall receive me, receiveth not me, but him that sent me. [Mark ix, 36, 37.]

And they brought unto him also infants, that he would touch them: but when his disciples saw it, they rebuked them. But Jesus called them unto him, and said, Suffer little children to come unto me, and forbid them not: for of such is the kingdom of God. Verily, I say unto you, Whosoever shall not receive the kingdom of God as a little child, shall in no wise enter therein. [Luke xviii, 15-17.]

FORM FOR THE BURIAL OF THE DEAD.

The Minister, going before the Corpse, shall say:

I AM the resurrection and the life : he that believeth in me, though he were dead, yet shall he live; and whosoever liveth, and believeth in me, shall never die. [John xi, 25, 26.]

I know that my Redeemer liveth, and that he shall stand at the latter day upon the earth: and though after my skin worms destroy this body, yet in my flesh shall I see God : whom I shall see for myself, and mine eyes shall behold, and not another.   [Job xix, 25–27.]

We brought nothing into this world, and it is certain we can carry nothing out.   The Lord gave and the Lord hath taken away : blessed be the name of the Lord. [1 Tim. vi, 7 ; Job i, 21.]

At the grave, when the Corpse is laid in the Earth, the Minister shall say:

Man that is born of a woman hath but a short time to live, and is full of misery.   He cometh up, and is cut down like a flower ; he fleeth as it were a shadow, and never continueth in one stay.

In the midst of life we are in death: of whom may we seek for succor, but of thee, O Lord, who for our sins art justly displeased ?

Yet, O Lord God most holy, O Lord most mighty, O holy and most merciful Saviour, deliver us not into the bitter pains of eternal death.

Thou knowest, Lord, the secrets of our hearts ; shut not thy merciful ears to our prayers, but spare us, Lord most holy, O God most mighty, O holy and merciful Saviour, thou most worthy Judge eternal, suffer us not at our last hour for any pains of death to fall from thee.

3

Then, while the Earth shall be cast upon the Body by some standing by, the Minister shall say:

Forasmuch as it hath pleased Almighty God, in his wise providence, to take out of the world the soul of the departed, we therefore commit *his* body to the ground ; earth to earth, ashes to ashes, dust to dust; looking for the general resurrection in the last day, and the life of the world to come, through our Lord Jesus Christ; at whose second coming in glorious majesty to judge the world, the earth and the sea shall give up their dead ; and the corruptible bodies of those who sleep in him shall be changed and made like unto his own glorious body, according to the mighty working whereby he is able to subdue all things unto himself.

Then shall be said :

I heard a voice from heaven saying unto me, Write, From henceforth blessed are the dead who die in the Lord : Even so, saith the Spirit; for they rest from their labors.

Then shall the Minister say:

Lord, have mercy upon us.
Christ, have mercy upon us.
Lord, have mercy upon us.

Then the Minister may offer this Prayer :

Almighty God, with whom do live the spirits of those who depart hence in the Lord, and with whom the souls of the faithful, after they are delivered from the burden of the flesh, are in joy and felicity; we give thee hearty thanks for the good examples of all those thy servants, who, having finished their course in faith, do now rest from their labors. And we beseech thee, that we, with all those who are departed in the true faith of thy holy

name, may have our perfect consummation and bliss'
both in body and soul, in thy eternal and everlasting
glory, through Jesus Christ our Lord. *Amen.*

The Collect.

O merciful God, the Father of our Lord Jesus Christ,
who is the resurrection and the life : in whom whosoever
believeth shall live, though he die, and whosoever liveth
and believeth in him shall not die eternally; we meekly
beseech thee, O Father, to raise us from the death of sin
into the life of righteousness ; that when we shall depart this life we may rest in him ; and at the general
resurrection on the last day may be found acceptable in
thy sight, and receive that blessing which thy well beloved Son shall then pronounce to all that love and fear
thee, saying, Come, ye blessed children of my Father,
receive the kingdom prepared for you from the beginning of the world. Grant this, we beseech thee, O merciful Father, through Jesus Christ our Mediator and
Redeemer. *Amen.*

Our Father who art in heaven, hallowed be thy name.
Thy kingdom come. Thy will be done in earth as it is
in heaven. Give us this day our daily bread ; and forgive us our trespasses as we forgive them that trespass
against us; and lead us not into temptation, but deliver
us from evil: for thine is the kingdom, and the power,
and the glory, forever. *Amen.*

The grace of our Lord Jesus Christ, and the love of
God, and the fellowship of the Holy Ghost, be with us
all evermore. *Amen.*

Statistical Blanks to the Annual Conference.

No. I.

CHURCH MEMBERSHIP.

No. of Probationers, ...
No. of Full Members, ...
No. of Local Preachers, ...
No. of Deaths, ...

BAPTISMS.

No. of Children, ...
No. of Adults, ...

SUNDAY SCHOOL.

No. of Schools, ...
No. of Officers and Teachers, ...
No. of Scholars, ...

CHURCH PROPERTY.

No. of Churches, ...
Probable Value, ... $ ....
No. of Parsonages, ...
Probable Value, ... $...............
Amount paid on Building and Improvements, ...
Amount paid on Old Indebtedness, ...
Present Indebtedness, ...

No. 2.

SUNDAY SCHOOL.

No. of Schools, ...
No. of Officers and Teachers, ...
No. of Scholars of all grades, ...
No. of Members in the Home Department, ...
Average Attendance, ...
No. of Officers and Teachers who are Church Members or
    Probationers, ...
No. of Scholars (whether attendants or members in the
    Home Department) who are Church Members or Pro-
    bationers, ...
No. of Members of Sunday School Converted during the year ....
Current Expenses, ...

No. 3.

PASTOR'S SUPPORT.

CLAIMS:
Salary, ... $..................
House Rent, ...

Total, . . . $ ....

RECEIPTS:
Salary, ... $..................
House Rent, ...

Total, ... $..................
Deficiencies, . . $..................

SUPPORT OF PRESIDING ELDERS.

Amount Apportioned, . . . $..................
Amount Paid, ...

SUPPORT OF BISHOPS.

Amount Apportioned. . . . $..................
Amount Paid, ...

Total Support Paid as above, . . $..................

CONFERENCE CLAIMANTS.

Received from Collections, ... $..................
Received from Other Sources, ...

Total Receipts, ... $..................

CURRENT EXPENSES.

CHURCH: Sexton, Light, Fuel, etc., ... $..................
SUNDAY SCHOOL: Lesson Leaves, Books, etc., ...

No. 4.

BENEVOLENT COLLECTIONS.

MISSIONARY SOCIETY:
    a. Church, . . $..................
    b. Sunday School, ... $..................
Church Extension, ...
Sunday School Union, ...
Tract Society, ...

Freedmen's Aid and Southern Education Society, . . $..... ....

EDUCATION:

    a. Public Educational Collection, $.................

    b. Children's Fund, ...

American Bible Society, ...

Woman's Foreign Missionary Society, ...

Woman's Home Missionary Society, ...

        Total Disciplinary Collections,   .   . $. ....

Other Benevolent Collections, . $.................

                ....

                ....,....

                ....

                ....

        Total Benevolent Collections, .   .   . $.................

General Conference Expenses, ...

Conference Claimants, ...

Episcopal Fund, ...

        Total,   .   . $.................

FINANCIAL REPORT FOR CONFERENCE TREASURER.

A duplicate of Statistical Blank No. 4, and is to be filled up, added, torn off, and handed, with cash, receipts, and the envelope, properly filled out, to the Treasurer.

COLLECTIONS.	CASH.	Receipts for Cash already Paid.	TOTAL.
Missionary Society......			
Church Extension			
Sunday School Union.................			
Tract Society.........................			
Freedmen's Aid and Southern Education Society......................			
EDUCATION:			
a. Public Educational Collection			
b. Children's Fund................			
American Bible Society..............			
Woman's Foreign Missionary Soc..			
Woman's Home Missionary Society.			
Other Benevolent Collections........			
General Conference Expenses.......			
Conference Claimants...............			
Episcopal Fund......................			
Total.................			

PASTOR'S REPORT
TO THE QUARTERLY CONFERENCE.

	1st Qr.	2d Qr.	3d Qr.	4th Qr.
I. Sunday School and Religious Instruction.				
1. No. of Sunday Schools......	......	......	......	......
2. State of the Schools......	......	......	......	......
3. Average Attendance......	......	......	......	......
4. No. Sermons Preached by the Pastor to Children......	......	......	......	......
5. No. of times Pastor has Catechised the Children......	......	......	......	......
6. No. of Classes of Children formed for Religious Instruction......	......	......	......	......
II. Changes in Membership.				
1. Admitted from Probation......	......	......	......	......
2. Received by Certificate......	......	......	......	......
3. Granted Certificates......	......	......	......	......
4. Deceased......	......	......	......	......
5. Withdrawn......	......	......	......	......
6. Excluded......	......	......	......	......
III. Pastoral Labor.				
1. No. of Pastoral Visits......	......	......	......	......
2. Other Items......	......	......	......	......
IV. Benevolent Collections.				
1. Missions......	......	......	......	......
2. Church Extension......	......	......	......	......
3. Education......	......	......	......	......
4. Freedmen's Aid and Southern Education......	......	......	......	......
5. Sunday Schools and Sunday School Union......	......	......	......	......
6. Tracts......	......	......	......	......
7. American Bible Society......	......	......	......	......
8. Other Objects......	......	......	......	......
V. Subscribers for our Periodicals.				
1. ......Christian Advocate......	......	......	......	......
2. Methodist Review......	......	......	......	......
3. Sunday School Journal......	......	......	......	......
4. Sunday School Advocate......	......	......	......	......
5. The Classmate......	......	......	......	......
6. Epworth Herald......	......	......	......	......
7. Other Periodicals......	......	......	......	......

PASTOR'S REPORT

TO THE QUARTERLY CONFERENCE.

I. Sunday School and Religious Instruction.	1st Qr.	2d Qr.	3d Qr.	4th Qr.
1. No. of Sunday Schools				
2. State of the Schools				
3. Average Attendance				
4. No. Sermons Preached by the Pastor to Children				
5. No. of times Pastor has Catechised the Children				
6. No. of Classes of Children formed for Religious Instruction				

II. Changes in Membership.

	1st Qr.	2d Qr.	3d Qr.	4th Qr.
1. Admitted from Probation				
2. Received by Certificate				
3. Granted Certificates				
4. Deceased				
5. Withdrawn				
6. Excluded				

III. Pastoral Labor.

	1st Qr.	2d Qr.	3d Qr.	4th Qr.
1. No. of Pastoral Visits				
2. Other Items				

IV. Benevolent Collections.

	1st Qr.	2d Qr.	3d Qr.	4th Qr.
1. Missions				
2. Church Extension				
3. Education				
4. Freedmen's Aid and Southern Education				
5. Sunday Schools and Sunday School Union				
6. Tracts				
7. American Bible Society				
8. Other Objects				

V. Subscribers for our Periodicals.

	1st Qr.	2d Qr.	3d Qr.	4th Qr.
1. .... Christian Advocate				
2. Methodist Review				
3. Sunday School Journal				
4. Sunday School Advocate				
5. The Classmate				
6. Epworth Herald				
7. Other Periodicals				

Time.	Name.	Place.

Time.	Name.	Place.

Text.	Place.

Time.	Text.	Place.

Time.	Text.	Place.

| Time. | Text. |

Time.	Text.	Place.

Time.	Text.	Place.

Time.	Text.	Place.

Names.	Residences.

Names. Residences.

Names.	Residences.

Names.   Residences.

Names.	Residences.

Names. **Residences.**

Names.	Residences.

Names.	Residences.

Names.	Residences.

Names.	Residences.

Names.	Residences.

Names.	Residences.

Names.	Residences.

Names.	Residences.

Names.	Residences.

Names.   Residences.

Names.	Residences.

Names.	Residences.

Names.	Residences.

Names.	Residences.

Names.	Residences.

Names.	Residences.

ALPHABETICAL LIST OF MEMBERS.

Names.	Residences.

Names.	Residences.

Names.	Residences.

ALPHABETICAL LIST OF PROBATIONERS.

When Received.	Names.	Residences.

When Received.	Names.	Residences.

ALPHABETICAL LIST OF PROBATIONERS.

When Received.	Names.	Residences.

When Received.	Names.	Residences.

When Received.	Names.	Residences.

When Received.	Names.	Residences.

When Received.	Names.	Residences.

When Received.	Names.	Residences.

When Received.	Names.	Residences.

When Received.	Names.	Residences.

When Received.	Names.	Residences.

Names.	Residences.

Names.   Residences.

Names.   Residences.

Names.   Residences,

ALPHABETICAL LIST OF FRIENDS NOT MEMBERS.

Names.	Residences.

Names.	Residences.

Names.	Residences.

Names.	Residences.

Time.	Name.	Father's Name.

Mother's Name.	When Born.	Remarks.

Time.	Name.	Father's Name.

Mother's Name.	When Born.	Remarks.

RECORD OF

Time.	Name.	Father's Name.

Mother's Name.	When Born.	Remarks.

Time.	Names.	Father's Name.

Mother's Name.	When Born.	Remarks.

Time.	Names.	Residences.

Remarks.   Fee.

| Time. | Names. | Residences. |

Remarks. **Fee.**

RECORD OF

Time.   Names.   Residences.

Remarks.   Fee.

RECORD OF

Time.	Names.	Residences.

Remarks.   **Fee.**

Periodical. Subscriber's Name.

When to End.	Where to be Sent.	Am't Paid.

SUBSCRIBERS FOR

Periodical.	Subscriber's Name.	When to Beg:

When to End.	Where to be Sent.	Am't Paid.

Periodical.	Subscriber's Name.	When to Begin

When to End.	Where to be Sent.	Am't Paid.

Periodical.	Subscriber's Name.	When to Begi

When to End.	Where to be Sent.	Am't Paid.

CASH ACCOUNT.

Date.	Names.	Received.	Paid.

Date.	Names.	Received.	Paid.

CASH ACCOUNT.

Date.	Names.	Received.	Paid.

Date.	Names.	Received.	Paid.

GENERAL MEMORANDA.

GENERAL MEMORANDA.

GENERAL MEMORANDA.

GENERAL MEMORANDA.

GENERAL MEMORANDA.

GENERAL MEMORANDA.

GENERAL MEMORANDA.

GENERAL MEMORANDA.

DIARY, 18

DIARY, 18

DIARY, 18

DIARY, 18

DIARY, 18

DIARY, 18

DIARY, 18

DIARY, 18

DIARY, 18

DIARY, 18

DIARY, 18

DIARY, 18

DIARY, 18

DIARY, 18

DIARY, 18

www.ingramcontent.com/pod-product-compliance
Lightning Source LLC
Chambersburg PA
CBHW020540270326
41927CB00006B/655